Editorial Project Manager
Erica N. Russikoff, M.A.

Editor in Chief
Brent L. Fox, M. Ed.

Creative Director
Sarah M. Fournier

Cover Artist
Diem Pascarella

Illustrator
Crystal-Dawn Keitz

Imaging
Amanda R. Harter

Publisher
Mary D. Smith, M.S. Ed.

Teacher Created Resources

Author
Samantha Chagollan

Teacher Created Resources
12621 Western Avenue
Garden Grove, CA 92841
www.teachercreated.com
ISBN: 978-1-4206-8309-7
©2020 Teacher Created Resources
Reprinted, 2021
Made in U.S.A.

Teacher Created Resources

TABLE OF CONTENTS

INTRODUCTION

In 1988, a group of researchers, including Stanford psychology professor Carol Dweck, studied students' responses to failure.

Some students rebounded well, while others were derailed by simple setbacks.

After extensive research with thousands of students, Dr. Dweck came up with the terms *fixed mindset* and *growth mindset* to encapsulate the differences between how all of us think about learning.

Simply put, having a growth mindset means you believe that you can and will improve with effort. A fixed mindset, by comparison, means that you believe you have a fixed amount of intelligence or talent that will never change.

We all have these two mindsets, but what Dr. Dweck has shown is that students are more likely to succeed once they take on a growth mindset and understand that they can get better at anything with time and effort.

In a fixed mindset, challenges are avoided, criticism is ignored, and students feel threatened by the success of others and are quick to give up when things get hard.

In a growth mindset, mistakes are seen as learning opportunities, challenges are welcomed, and students persevere with effort, leading to a desire to learn even more.

Teaching students about a growth mindset and the science behind it, including brain plasticity, has helped countless students grasp the idea that they can achieve their dreams, no matter their starting points.

The activities in this book support the growth-mindset philosophy. With practice and positive reinforcement, students will be able to adopt this flexible, supportive, and uplifting perspective.

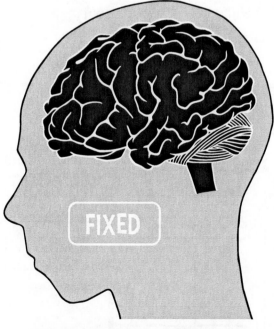

knowledge is unchanging

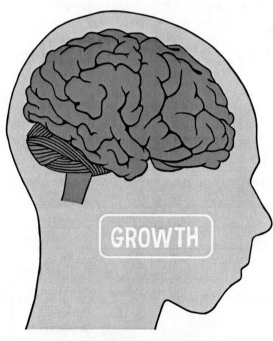

knowledge can grow

HOW TO USE THIS BOOK

For practical application in the classroom, this book provides 12 units that are each focused on one of the following growth-mindset mantras:

- ⭐ I will do my best.
- ⭐ I can put in more time and effort.
- ⭐ I can learn from my mistakes.
- ⭐ I believe I can do it.
- ⭐ I can reach my goals.
- ⭐ I am not afraid of difficult tasks.

- ⭐ I can come up with creative solutions.
- ⭐ I can improve with practice.
- ⭐ I value thoughtful feedback.
- ⭐ I am capable of learning new things.
- ⭐ I can keep going when things are tough.
- ⭐ I can train my brain.

Each unit includes an overview for the teacher and six student activities to support each mantra.

Reading Passage: To help students understand the meaning of the mantra, each unit includes a nonfiction narrative that features the story of someone who exemplifies that mantra.

Short-Answer Activity: After reading, students are asked a handful of questions that will check for understanding and provide potential talking points for a larger class discussion about the mantra.

Small-Group Activity: Students are asked to gather in small groups and collaborate to gain a deeper understanding.

Whole-Class Activity: The class is asked to reflect on their learning together; whole-class activities provide a perfect forum for learning about growth-mindset principles and practices, too.

Journal Prompt: Students are given the opportunity to reflect on what they have learned in the unit.

Growing Beyond: An extension activity is presented to take learning beyond the classroom for deeper understanding. *Note:* This activity is listed on the lesson plan and does not have its own page.

All the activities in this book have been aligned to the Common Core State Standards (CCSS). A correlations chart is included on pages 79–80.

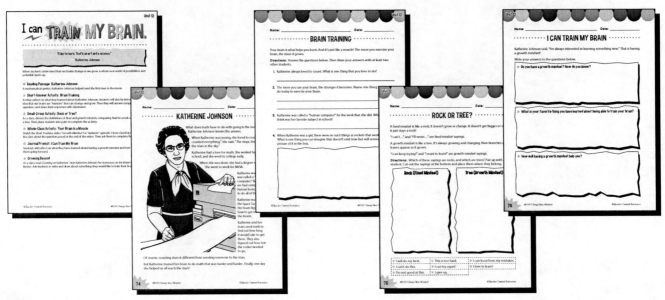

TEACHER SELF-ASSESSMENT

Before you dive into teaching growth mindset, it's a good idea to know where you stand.

Read each statement and note whether this is something you always, sometimes, or never do or say. On a separate piece of paper, take notes that might be helpful for your own self-reflection.

		Always	Sometimes	Never
1.	I am inspired when others around me succeed.	☐	☐	☐
2.	I believe that intelligence can improve.	☐	☐	☐
3.	I learn from my mistakes.	☐	☐	☐
4.	When things get challenging, I am likely to give up.	☐	☐	☐
5.	If something doesn't work, I try a different strategy.	☐	☐	☐
6.	I receive feedback and criticism well.	☐	☐	☐
7.	There are some things I am just not good at.	☐	☐	☐
8.	I set goals and monitor my progress.	☐	☐	☐
9.	I have a set way of doing things that works for me.	☐	☐	☐
10.	Some students just aren't good at certain things.	☐	☐	☐
11.	I love to learn new things.	☐	☐	☐
12.	I notice when I am thinking negative thoughts, and I am able to change those thoughts to more encouraging ones.	☐	☐	☐

We all fluctuate between both fixed and growth mindsets, but it's important to know for yourself which side you favor.

In this assessment, items 4, 7, 9, and 10 are fixed-mindset statements. The rest are growth-mindset statements.

Each mantra featured in this book is a growth-mindset statement that you can reinforce in your classroom. The more you use and model these mantras for your students, the greater their understanding of the growth mindset will be.

PARENT LETTER

As you're teaching your students about growth mindset, bring parents into the picture so this attitude can be practiced at home, too.

Consider creating a parent letter that explains what the growth mindset is, and how parents can support their child's learning. Here's an example:

Dear Parents,

Many of us grew up believing that either we were smart or we weren't. We were either good at something or we weren't.

But now, through scientific research, we know that simply isn't true. Our brains can grow and change, and when students are aware of this, they can get inspired to learn more.

I'm working with your child to help develop a "growth mindset." Someone with a growth mindset gives their best effort, learns from mistakes, and finds creative solutions to problems.

I would love for you to help support this growth mindset at home, too. Here are some ideas for how you can help:

★ Remind your child that mistakes are okay. We all make them! Each time we try and fail, our brains get stronger, and this is how we learn to persevere when things get tough.

★ Praise effort over achievement. It's the process that counts, so compliment your child for the work they put in, the creativity they displayed, or the determination they showed.

★ Ask questions like, "How were you challenged today? What mistakes did you make? What did you learn?"

★ Help your child practice growth-mindset self-talk. If you hear your child say something like, "I can't do this!" have them try saying, "I can't do this yet, but I'll keep trying."

The more you can talk about this and model it for your child, the more they will understand that intelligence can change and achievement is never out of reach when effort is given.

Thank you for your support!

I will DO MY BEST.

> "Start unknown, finish unforgettable."
>
> Misty Copeland

When students understand the importance of giving their best effort to a challenge, they begin to see the possibilities of what they can achieve.

★ Reading Passage: Misty Copeland

Ballerina Misty Copeland overcame a challenging childhood to become the most famous dancer of her generation.

★ Short-Answer Activity: The Best You Can Be

Read the short poem aloud to the class; discuss what it means to do your best. Then ask students to answer the questions about what they read.

★ Small-Group Activity: Best of Friends

Students will pair up and interview each other about what they are best at, as well as some of their favorite things. When done, ask students to share and introduce their partners to the class.

★ Whole-Class Activity: Best Foot Forward

In this movement activity, students will complete a short matching task and then perform a silly movement they will share with the class.

★ Journal Prompt: Doing Your Best

Reflecting on what they have learned, students will draw or write about a time they were proud of giving their best.

★ Growing Beyond

Send students home with a plain lunch bag. Ask them to choose three things that represent the best of themselves and place the objects in the bag. The only rule is that the objects must fit in the bag. They can also decorate the bag however they would like. For a week, designate some time each day for a small group of students to share their "best of me" bags with the class.

Name: _____   **Date:** _____

MISTY COPELAND

Misty Copeland is a famous ballet dancer. Her story shows us that dreams can come true.

Most dancers start training when they are young. But Misty didn't find ballet until she was 13 years old.

Misty grew up with five brothers and sisters. She moved around a lot. She was shy. And she always wanted to be perfect.

In middle school, she was on the drill team. Misty loved gymnastics. Her teacher thought she might like to try ballet.

Misty loved dance right away. She was good at it, too! She began training as much as she could.

"I can do anything when I am in a tutu," she said. Misty knew she wanted to give her all to dance.

The more Misty trained, the better she danced. She wanted to be the best she could be. She never gave up, even when it was hard.

Misty just kept practicing. Then she joined the American Ballet Theatre. She was the first black woman to be a star dancer.

Misty has inspired dancers all over the world. She is a true example of what it means to do your best.

Name: _____ **Date:** _____

THE BEST YOU CAN BE

Doing your best means giving your all. Here is a poem about what it means to do your best.

Your Best

If you always try your best
Then you'll never have to wonder
About what you could have done
If you'd summoned all your thunder.

And if your best
Was not as good
As you hoped it would be,
You still could say,
"I gave today
All that I had in me."

—Barbara R. Vance, from *Suzie Bitner Was Afraid of the Drain*

Directions: Think about Misty's story and the poem above. Then answer the questions below.

1. What does it feel like when you do your best? _____

   _____

2. What could stop you from doing your best? _____

   _____

   _____

3. What are three words you would use to describe Misty? _____

   _____

Name: _____ **Date:** _____

BEST OF FRIENDS

Directions: Find a partner. Ask them these questions about their best and favorite things. Write or draw their answers below.

⭐ **What is your friend's name?** ⭐

⭐ **What is your friend best at?** ⭐

⭐ **Who is your friend's best friend?** ⭐

⭐ **What is your friend's favorite memory?** ⭐

Name: _____ **Date:** _____

BEST FOOT FORWARD

Directions: There are three parts to this activity. Look at the two lists below.

★ First, draw lines matching a descriptive word from the left side of the page with a movement on the right side. You can match up any word from the left with any word on the right.

★ Choose one of the silly movement pairs you made and write it on the line below.

★ Then, when your teacher says it's time, perform your movement for the class. Do your best!

Descriptive Words	Movement Words
Groovy	Hop
Robot	Spin
Sleepy	Jump
Ballerina	Walk
Wavy	Turn
Weird	Bend
Stiff	Skip

My silly movement is _____.

Name: _____   **Date:** _____

· · · · · · · · · · · · · DOING YOUR BEST · · · · · · · · · · · · ·

When you do your best, you can be proud of your efforts. Can you think of a time when you did your best? Were you proud of yourself? What were you doing, and how did it feel? Draw or write your answers below.

I can PUT IN MORE TIME and EFFORT.

> "I've failed over and over and over again in my life, and that is why I succeed."
>
> Michael Jordan

Big goals can become achievable with dedicated time and effort. In this unit, students will discover the incredible results of hard work and dedication.

★ Reading Passage: Michael Jordan

Some call him the greatest basketball player of all time, but it's his work ethic and determination to improve that make Michael Jordan a true champion.

★ Short-Answer Activity: Great Effort

In pairs, students will talk about what they learned from Michael Jordan. Individually, they will answer short comprehension questions about the reading passage.

★ Small-Group Activity: Your Best

Students will fill out a self-assessment about level of effort and then get into small groups to discuss their answers. Bring the class back together to talk about what they discovered. Are the activities they like the ones they give more effort to? What would it be like if they gave more effort to the activities that are harder?

★ Whole-Class Activity: Master This

Students will draw something they would like to master and then share it with the class. When finished, consider creating a bulletin board of the drawings they create, or create a poster of all the things they want to master.

★ Journal Prompt: Giving Your Best

Reflecting on something they worked hard at today, students will draw a picture and write about giving their best effort.

★ Growing Beyond

As a class, watch the short YouTube video "Things You Might Not Know About Michael Jordan." Ask students to choose one of the five achievements presented in the video and draw a picture of Michael Jordan achieving that goal. Discuss as a class.

Name: _____ **Date:** _____

· · · · · · · · · MICHAEL JORDAN · · · · · · · · ·

Michael Jordan is a legend. He is a famous basketball player who is known all over the world. But it took a lot of hard work for him to reach his dreams.

When Michael was young, he was still learning how to play. He didn't know how to dunk. And he wasn't as tall as some of the other kids in his grade. That meant he had to work even harder than everyone else.

Michael tried out for his high school's basketball team. But when the team list was posted, his name was not on it.

He was disappointed. But he picked himself up and kept going. Michael knew he had to work harder to make the team.

"Whenever I was working out and got tired…I'd close my eyes and see that list…without my name on it," Michael said. "That usually got me going again."

That summer, Michael put in extra effort. He trained even harder. The next year, he made the team. He became the team's best player!

Michael became a great player in college. Then he became a pro. He set records with the Chicago Bulls. Michael was voted Most Valuable Player, too.

Some people say Michael is the greatest basketball player ever.

He said, "I've always believed that if you put in the work, the results will come."

Name: _____   **Date:** _____

GREAT EFFORT

Michael has said, "If you do the work, you get rewarded. There are no shortcuts in life."

Now that you have read Michael Jordan's story, think about what you learned.

Directions: Find a partner. Talk about your favorite part of Michael's story. Then, on your own, answer the questions below.

1. How do you think Michael felt when he didn't make the team? Have you ever felt like that?

   _____

   _____

2. What did Michael do when he didn't make the team? _____

   _____

3. What is one thing you learned from reading about Michael? _____

   _____

   _____

4. Draw a picture of yourself doing something you love to do. How much effort are you giving?

Name: _____ **Date:** _____

• • • • • • • • • • • • • • • • • YOUR BEST • • • • • • • • • • • • • • • •

What does it mean to give your best effort?

It means you try hard and give your all. Even when—especially when—the thing you're doing is hard.

Directions: On your own, rate the amount of effort you give to the activities in the table. Color in the boxes that match your level of effort.

Then form a group with two other students. Talk about your answers. Are they alike? Are the activities that you like the ones you give the most effort to?

Activity	Small Effort (I try, but I give up when it gets hard.)	Good Effort (I could do more.)	Awesome Effort (I do my very best.)
Art			
Exercise			
Listening			
Math			
Music			
Reading			
Science			
Social Studies			

#8309 Change Your Mindset

Name: _____   **Date:** _____

MASTER THIS

Have you ever heard that it takes 10,000 hours of study to become a master at something? That is a lot of effort! But the effort is worth it if it's your dream.

Directions: What is something you would like to master? Draw a picture below. Then share it with the class.

Name: _____ **Date:** _____

· · · · · · · · · · · # GIVING YOUR BEST · · · · · · · · · · · ·

As Michael Jordan says, trying to do your best is the best you can do.

What is one thing you tried hard at today? Draw a picture of how you gave your best effort. Then write about it on the lines below.

_____

_____

_____

_____

_____

_____

I can LEARN from my MISTAKES.

> "Many of life's failures are people who did not realize how close they were to success when they gave up."
>
> — Thomas Edison

Failure is just a part of learning, and mistakes are opportunities to grow. In this unit, students will understand the value of mistakes and how they can help on the journey to success.

★ Reading Passage: Thomas Edison

The most well-known inventor in history made incredible things; he also failed many times over.

★ Short-Answer Activity: Learning from Mistakes

After reading about Thomas Edison, students will answer comprehension questions about the passage.

★ Small-Group Activity: We Made This!

Break students up into small groups. Provide basic materials, such as plastic cups, spaghetti, pipe cleaners, marshmallows, and tape. Ask students to invent something together, write about it individually, and present their invention to the class.

★ Whole-Class Activity: Beautiful Oops!

As a class, read *Beautiful Oops!* by Barney Saltzberg. Discuss how making a "mistake" can actually be inspiration for creativity. Tell students to close their eyes, make a mark on the page, and turn it into something different.

★ Journal Prompt: Taught by Mistake

Students will reflect on learning from mistakes, especially those mistakes that have taught them lessons.

★ Growing Beyond

Look up "inventions by mistake" online. Discuss as a class all of the incredible inventions that almost never were because they were mistakes.

Name: _____ **Date:** _____

THOMAS EDISON

Thomas Edison is a famous inventor. He was a scientist who had many great, new ideas.

As a boy, he liked to take things apart. He would see how they worked. Then he would put all the parts back together again.

Thomas was 10 years old when he set up his first lab. He liked to try out his ideas to see if they would work.

When he was 12, he learned how to use a telegraph.

Before we had phones, we used telegraphs. Telegraphs helped us talk to one another from far away.

When Thomas grew up, he invented his own telegraph.

Soon, he was inventing all kinds of things. Thomas made a machine that could record and play back sound. This was called a *phonograph*.

He also made the first motion-picture machine. If it hadn't been for Thomas, we wouldn't have movies!

Thomas made lightbulbs that could be used at home. He thought up the first x-ray machine. And he created so much more! We still use many of his ideas today.

But along the way, he made a lot of mistakes. He said, "I have not failed. I've just found 10,000 ways that won't work."

Mistakes did not stop Thomas. Each mistake helped him learn something new. That is how he became the most famous inventor in history.

Name: _____   **Date:** _____

· · · · · · · · LEARNING FROM MISTAKES · · · · · · · ·

Thomas Edison had to make a lot of mistakes as he invented his creations. But he never thought of mistakes as bad—he knew that each mistake was just giving him a chance to learn.

Directions: Think about what you learned about Thomas Edison. Then answer the questions below.

1. Name one of Thomas Edison's inventions. Why do you think it is important?

   _____

   _____

   _____

2. What did Thomas Edison like to do when he was young?

   _____

   _____

3. If you could, what is one question you would ask Thomas Edison?

   _____

   _____

4. If you could invent anything, what would you make? Draw it in the box.

Name: _____ Date: _____

• • • • • • • • • • • • • WE MADE THIS! • • • • • • • • • • • • •

What can you invent? Just like Thomas Edison, you may make some mistakes along the way, but stick with it. You might invent something great!

Directions: Form a group with two or three other students. Using the materials you are given, work with your group to create an invention. Be ready to share your invention with the class. Then, on your own, write your answers to the questions below.

★ What did you invent? ★

★ What is your invention named? ★

★ What does it do? ★

★ How does it work? ★

Name: _____   **Date:** _____

· · · · · · · · · BEAUTIFUL OOPS! · · · · · · · · ·

In the book *Beautiful Oops!*, we learn that every "mistake" is the beginning of something new.

Directions: When your teacher tells you to, close your eyes and make a mark somewhere on this page. No peeking!

Open your eyes and turn that mark into a picture. What do you see? What happens if you turn the page upside down and look at it a different way?

Name: _____   **Date:** _____

· · · · · · · · · · · TAUGHT BY MISTAKE · · · · · · · · · · · ·

Mistakes are proof that you are trying. If you mess up, at least you know you are making an effort!

Think about what you learned from Thomas Edison's story and *Beautiful Oops!* What have you discovered about making mistakes?

Can you think of a mistake you have made? What did you learn from it?

_____

_____

_____

_____

_____

_____

_____

_____

_____

_____

_____

_____

_____

_____

_____

_____

I BELIEVE I can DO IT.

> "With my life, I want to use my voice to be able to reach out to as many people and inspire others to make a difference."
>
> Bindi Irwin

As students build confidence in themselves, they are willing to take on greater challenges and soar.

★ Reading Passage: Bindi Irwin

After Bindi Irwin's famous wildlife expert father, Steve Irwin, passed away, she had to find inner strength to go on.

★ Short-Answer Activity: I Believe in Myself

In pairs, students will talk about what they learned from Bindi Irwin. Individually, they will answer short comprehension questions about the reading passage.

★ Small-Group Activity: Reflection of Me

To work on building confidence, students will compliment one another and then practice giving themselves compliments, too. If possible, have hand mirrors available for students to use when they read the compliments back to themselves.

★ Whole-Class Activity: Words of Encouragement

Building on the last activity, students will recall some of the positive words they heard about themselves. Ask them to share, and create a word-cloud poster or bulletin board that will serve as an affirming reminder to the class.

★ Journal Prompt: I Can Do Anything

After reading Bindi's story and learning about self-confidence, students will reflect on how it feels to believe in yourself.

★ Growing Beyond

Create a "Confidence Jar" for your classroom. Record positive growth-mindset affirmations on slips of paper, and let students know they can come pick one out on days when they are feeling less confident.

Name: _____   Date: _____

BINDI IRWIN

Do you know anyone who grew up in a zoo? Bindi Irwin did! Bindi and her family take care of wild animals.

Since she was a baby, she has lived in a zoo. Her job is to take care of the animals. To Bindi, it is the best job in the world!

She loves spiders and snakes as much as koalas and kangaroos. Bindi is friends with all of the animals.

Bindi is just like her famous dad, Steve Irwin. He had his own TV show called *The Crocodile Hunter*.

On his show, Steve taught us why animals mean so much to our planet. His dream was for people to love them as much as he did.

Bindi's dad taught her so much. She got to be on his TV show with him. And she found out that when people learned more about animals, they wanted to save them, too.

Sadly, when Bindi was eight years old, her dad died. Bindi and her mom and brother had to figure out what to do without him.

Bindi wanted to follow in her dad's footsteps. She knew her dad would want her to believe in herself.

She started her own TV show called *Bindi: The Jungle Girl*.

On her show, she rode an elephant. She cuddled a koala. She even held a python. And she helped teach viewers about wildlife all over the world.

Bindi is still happiest when she is at home in the zoo. Because she believes in herself, she knows she can do anything.

Name: _____   **Date:** _____

· · · · · · · · · · · · · I BELIEVE IN MYSELF · · · · · · · · · · · ·

Directions: Find a partner. Think about what you read about Bindi Irwin. Then talk about these questions together:

★ Do you think Bindi ever felt like giving up after her dad was gone?

★ Why do you think she decided to make her own show?

Directions: On your own, answer the questions below.

1. Bindi had to have confidence in herself to carry on her dad's legacy. What are some other words you would use to describe Bindi?

   _____

   _____

2. Name something you admire about Bindi. _____

   _____

3. What is something you have done that you are proud of? _____

   _____

4. Draw a picture of your answer to #3 in the box.

Name: _____ **Date:** _____

• • • • • • • • • • • REFLECTION OF ME • • • • • • • • • • •

Directions: Form a group with two other students. Sit in a circle. One at a time, turn to the person on your right and give them a compliment.

When you get a compliment, write it inside the mirror.

Then go back around the circle the other way. Write that compliment, too.

Your turn! Write at least two more compliments to yourself on the mirror.

When you're done, practice picking up the mirror and reading the compliments back to yourself. Say each one with confidence!

Name: _____ **Date:** _____

·········· WORDS OF ENCOURAGEMENT ········

Sometimes, your confidence is low. It can help to think about some positive words. It will help you remember to believe in yourself!

What are some of the compliments you have received? What about the nice things that other people say to you? What are some positive things you say to yourself?

Directions: In the box below, write some words that help you believe in the power of you. When you're done, share some of the words with the class. Together, you can create a classroom poster that shows all the positive things about your class!

Name: _____   **Date:** _____

· · · · · · · · · · · · I CAN DO ANYTHING · · · · · · · · · · ·

When we believe in ourselves, anything is possible.

Think about Bindi's story. Now, think about how you believe in yourself. Write your answers to the questions below.

⭐ What if you could do anything? What would you do?

⭐ How does it feel to believe in yourself?

_____

_____

_____

_____

_____

_____

_____

_____

_____

_____

_____

_____

_____

I can REACH my GOALS.

> "Always shoot for the sun and you will shine."
>
> Kwame Alexander

When students learn how to set goals, they begin to understand the possibilities of what they can achieve with effort and dedication.

★ Reading Passage: Kwame Alexander

After having his manuscript rejected 22 times, Kwame Alexander found a publisher and won the Newbery Medal for his breakthrough book.

★ Short-Answer Activity: Big Dreams

After reading Kwame's story, students will answer comprehension questions and start to think about their own goals.

★ Small-Group Activity: Stars & Wishes

In small groups, students will define what they are good at and what they wish they could improve. Once the groups have completed the activity, bring the class back together to talk about how they can help support one another in the areas that need improvement.

★ Whole-Class Activity: Go for the Goal

As a class, discuss the questions presented in the activity. Then ask students to complete the activity, defining their own goals. When complete, ask for volunteers to share their goals with the class and talk about what steps they will take to achieve them, as well as who can support them with their plans.

★ Journal Prompt: Reaching for the Stars

Students will reflect on what they learned, journaling and drawing about how it will feel to achieve their goals.

★ Growing Beyond

Create a bulletin board that will stay up all year, featuring each student's goal. On colorful bursts of paper, have students write the goals they've defined in these activities. Title the bulletin board "Watch Us Shine." Schedule regular check-ins throughout the year to ensure students are on track to reach their goals and have the support they need.

Name: _____   **Date:** _____

KWAME ALEXANDER

Kwame Alexander has always loved to read. There were so many books in his house, they were stacked all over the place.

He read every book he could. But, in fourth grade, things changed. Kwame decided he hated books.

Kwame didn't like any of the books he read. So he played sports instead. And a few years later, he found a book about sports that he liked.

Kwame never thought he would become a writer. He liked to write poetry. But that was just for fun.

In college, one of his teachers told him to write more poems. Kwame began to write a lot. He decided to write a book. His goal was to write the book he wished he'd had when he was young.

Kwame wrote a book called *The Crossover*. It's about two brothers and basketball. It's different from the way other books are written. It's kind of like a poem or a song.

No one had ever seen a book like *The Crossover* before. It was hard for Kwame to get anyone to read it. In fact, 22 different book publishers turned him down.

But Kwame didn't give up on his goal. And someone did read his book. They wanted to publish it.

The Crossover became a huge hit. Kwame won many awards for writing it. Now, Kwame publishes his own books and other books he likes. He did this so that kids everywhere can have fun books to read.

Name: _____   **Date:** _____

· · · · · · · · · · · · · · · · · · **BIG DREAMS** · · · · · · · · · · · · · · · ·

Goals are dreams we have for ourselves. With some effort, we can achieve our goals.

Directions: Think about what you read about Kwame Alexander. Then answer the questions below.

1. What was Kwame's goal? Did he achieve it? _____

   _____

   _____

2. What was the topic of the book that changed Kwame's mind about books?

   _____

3. Did Kwame give up when no one wanted to publish his book? How do you know?

   _____

   _____

4. If you wrote a book, what would it be about? Draw a picture that shows the main idea of your book.

Name: _____   Date: _____

· · · · · · · · · · · · STARS & WISHES · · · · · · · · · · · ·

When we set goals, we focus on what we need to improve. But first, we focus on what we are already doing well!

Stars are the things you are good at. **Wishes** are the things you would like to improve.

Directions: Form a group with two or three other students. On your own, answer the questions below. Then share your answers with your group.

What are three things you are good at?

What are three things you wish you could do better?

Name: _____   **Date:** _____

GO FOR THE GOAL

To reach your goals, you have to be clear on what you want.

Ask yourself these questions:

- ★ What exactly do I want to do?
- ★ Can I really do it?
- ★ Why is it important to me?
- ★ When will I have it done?
- ★ How will I know if I have done it?
- ★ Who will help me reach my goal?

Directions: Create a goal for yourself below. Then share it with the class.

★ My Goal ★

I will _____

_____

_____

by _____ .
(date)

I will reach my goal by _____

_____

_____

_____ .

Name: _____ **Date:** _____

· · · · · · · · REACHING FOR THE STARS · · · · · · · ·

How does it feel to have a goal? Think about why your goal matters to you. Why do you want it?

Now, imagine what it will be like when you achieve your goal. How will you feel? Who will be there with you? What will you be doing?

Write three sentences about how it will feel to achieve your goal. Then draw a picture of how you will feel.

_____

_____

_____

_____

_____

I am NOT afraid of DIFFICULT TASKS.

> "Learn from yesterday, live for today, hope for tomorrow.
> The important thing is not to stop questioning."
>
> ~ Albert Einstein

Facing difficulties is never easy, but students can learn to face challenges with bravery to help propel them toward success.

★ Reading Passage: Albert Einstein

The most famous genius in the world faced challenges, too—from early speech difficulties to college entrance.

★ Short-Answer Activity: Challenged to Grow

Students will reflect on what they have learned about Albert Einstein and the challenges he faced. Then they will answer comprehension questions.

★ Small-Group Activity: Have Some Courage

Students will write short stories about people who were brave. Then they will share their stories in small groups and answer questions.

★ Whole-Class Activity: Being Brave

Students will rate their reactions to challenging situations. Then they will discuss each one as a class. Ask students, "What is hard about this?" and discuss when and why courage is needed to face each difficulty.

★ Journal Prompt: Superhero Style

Imagining they are superheroes, students will journal and draw about what it would be like to have courage as a superpower.

★ Growing Beyond

As a class, read Jennifer Berne's book *On a Beam of Light: A Story of Albert Einstein* to discover more about the life of Albert Einstein. Afterward, discuss these questions as a class:

- ★ How did Albert overcome his difficulties?
- ★ How did Albert's curiosity help him?
- ★ What does it mean to be a genius?

Name: _____   **Date:** _____

ALBERT EINSTEIN

Albert Einstein was a famous thinker. He was a very smart scientist. Some even call him a genius!

But when Albert was a boy, no one thought he was very smart. He didn't speak very much. And he had a hard time in school.

When he got older, Albert asked a lot of questions. He was curious. He wondered how things worked.

One subject Albert liked was math. He also liked science. His favorite toy was a compass he got from his father. Albert was puzzled by the way it moved.

He also loved to play the violin. He said that playing music helped him think.

But school was not Albert's favorite place. Even though he was very smart, it was hard for him. He didn't get into college the first time he tried.

But Albert never gave up. He just worked a little bit harder.

And he kept asking questions. He was still curious. That's how he learned!

Albert finished school, and he wanted to be a teacher. But he couldn't find a job. So he became a scientist. He started writing about some of his ideas.

Some magazines printed his ideas. Soon, everyone was saying that Albert was a genius.

Albert became famous for his ideas. He is known as one of the smartest people who ever lived.

Name: _____   Date: _____

· · · · · · · · · · CHALLENGED TO GROW · · · · · · · · ·

Albert Einstein may have been a genius, but he still faced some challenges.

Directions: After reading Albert's story, answer the questions below.

1. What is one of the challenges that Albert faced? _____

_____

_____

2. Do you think Albert's challenges made him stronger? Why do you think this?

_____

_____

3. How did Albert deal with the challenges he faced? _____

_____

_____

4. What is something you have in common with Albert? Draw a picture of it in the box.

Name: _____   **Date:** _____

· · · · · · · · · · HAVE SOME COURAGE · · · · · · · · · ·

When someone is brave, we say they have *courage*. When you have courage, it means you are not afraid. You can face anything!

Directions: Write a story about someone who was brave.

_____

_____

_____

_____

_____

_____

Directions: Get into a group with three or four other students. Share your story with your group. Listen to their stories, too. Then answer the questions below about what you learned.

1. What was your favorite story of courage? _____

_____

_____

2. What did you like about it? _____

_____

_____

3. What does *courage* mean to you? _____

_____

_____

Name: _____   **Date:** _____

• • • • • • • • • • • • • • BEING BRAVE • • • • • • • • • • • • • • •

Directions: As a class, read these situations (things that happen). Then decide how you would react.

Rate and circle how it would make you feel. Use this scale:

1	**2**	**3**
I'm okay.	This bothers me a little.	I'm really upset.

1. The book you are reading has many new words in it.

   Rating: **1**   **2**   **3**

2. Your favorite after-school activity is canceled for a week.

   Rating: **1**   **2**   **3**

3. Your best friend has a new friend to sit with at lunch.

   Rating: **1**   **2**   **3**

4. There is a new vegetable on your dinner plate. You have never tried it before.

   Rating: **1**   **2**   **3**

5. You're invited to a birthday party for someone you just met.

   Rating: **1**   **2**   **3**

Name: _____ **Date:** _____

SUPERHERO STYLE

Imagine that you are a superhero. Your superpower is courage! You can do anything because you are always brave. How would you handle challenges?

Write three sentences about what you would do. Draw a picture that shows what it would be like to have courage as a superpower.

_____

_____

_____

_____

_____

I can COME ★ UP with CREATIVE SOLUTIONS.

> "You don't give people what they want.
> You give them what they don't yet know they want."
>
> Mo Willems

When the going gets tough, the tough get creative. By encouraging students to look for creative solutions to challenges, we empower them to find their own way through difficulties.

★ Reading Passage: Mo Willems

Creator of the unique and funny Pigeon series, and Elephant and Piggie books, author Mo Willems uses creative humor to tell stories.

★ Short-Answer Activity: Creativity Counts

After reading about Mo Willems, students will answer reading comprehension questions and reflect on creativity with a drawing prompt.

★ Small-Group Activity: Linked Together

In small groups, students will have to work together creatively to make a paper chain. Give each small group a single piece of construction paper, a pair of scissors, and glue. Teamwork and creativity will be key!

★ Whole-Class Activity: Help Is on the Way!

As a class, read *Today I Will Fly!* by Mo Willems. Afterward, discuss Piggie's determination and creative solutions to her problem. Then direct students to the activity to reflect on what they learned and have them share their answers with the class.

★ Journal Prompt: Up, Down, or Around?

Students will think about how they would overcome an obstacle, and then use their creativity to draw a picture of their response.

★ Growing Beyond

Read the class another Mo Willems story, such as *The Pigeon Needs a Bath!* Ask students to create their own story for Piggie and Gerald, or Pigeon. They will need to draw the pictures and tell the story.

Name: _____ **Date:** _____

• • • • • • • • • • • • • • • • • MO WILLEMS • • • • • • • • • • • • • •

Mo Willems writes books for kids. His books are really funny! And they are unlike most other books for kids.

When Mo was a kid himself, he liked to draw cartoons. But not everyone liked his drawings. One teacher even tore up his art!

That didn't stop Mo. He kept drawing cartoons. One year, he drew a cartoon every single day. That's 365 drawings!

As he grew up, Mo kept drawing and writing. He was a writer for the TV show *Sesame Street*. Mo was very creative.

Mo had an idea to write his own book for kids. The book was about a pigeon that wanted to drive a bus.

Mo sent the book to some of his friends, just for fun. They really seemed to like it. Some kids read the book, too, and they liked it a lot.

Someone told Mo he should get his book published. He asked around, but no one wanted it. Everyone thought his pigeon book was kind of weird. It was so different, no one knew what to do with it!

Then Mo found someone who loved his pigeon book. She didn't want him to change anything about it. She thought it was perfect just the way it was. So she published it.

Mo's book *Don't Let the Pigeon Drive the Bus!* was a big hit. Kids everywhere loved it.

Today, Mo is still writing books for kids. And he still loves being creative.

Name: _____ **Date:** _____

CREATIVITY COUNTS

When things get hard, we have to get creative! Just like Mo, we can create our own solutions.

Directions: Think about what you learned about Mo Willems. Then answer the questions below.

1. What does it mean to be creative? Are you creative? _____

   _____

   _____

2. What was Mo Willems's first book about? _____

   _____

   _____

3. How do you think Mo felt when his art was torn up? _____

   _____

4. When you are being creative, how do you feel? Draw a picture of your answer in the box.

Name: _____ Date: _____

LINKED TOGETHER

Directions: Form a group with two or three other students. Your teacher will give you a piece of colored paper, a pair of scissors, and glue.

How long of a chain can you make together? Your goal is to make the longest chain of paper that you can. You can only use the one piece of paper you were given.

Follow these steps to make the chain:

1. Cut the paper into strips.

2. Glue one end of a strip to the other end, making a circle.

3. Link the next piece through. Glue it together. Repeat.

Tip: Before you start cutting, talk to one another. Discuss how to make the longest chain.

You may need to get creative! When you're done, let your teacher know.

Name: _____   **Date:** _____

· · · · · · · · · HELP IS ON THE WAY! · · · · · · · ·

In the book *Today I Will Fly!*, Piggie is determined to fly. She has to use her creativity to fly. Piggie's creative idea is to ask for help. The bird she meets helps her fly!

When things get hard, sometimes we need to ask for help.

Directions: Answer the questions below. Then share your answers with the class.

Who is someone you can ask for help? _____

What does this person help you with? _____

_____

_____

_____

Draw a picture of this person helping you.

Name: _____   **Date:** _____

· · · · · · · · · · · UP, DOWN, OR AROUND? · · · · · · · · ·

Imagine that you are walking along one day, and there is a huge rock in your way. It's so big, you can't even see around it.

What will you do? How will you get around the rock? Use your creative brain.

Draw a picture of yourself and the rock and what you would do.

I can IMPROVE with PRACTICE.

> "I'm someone who never thought I would end up in a career where I had to speak fluently. And here I am."
>
> Emily Blunt

Practicing a skill isn't about reaching perfection; it's about making progress. In this unit, students will learn how improvement comes in small steps.

★ Reading Passage: Emily Blunt

Overcoming a severe stutter took actress Emily Blunt years of practice, but ultimately practice helped her learn how to thrive.

★ Short-Answer Activity: You Can Improve

Reflecting on what they learned from the reading passage, students will answer comprehension questions.

★ Small-Group Activity: Balloon Tennis

Make paddles with paper plates and large craft sticks. Break the class into three or four small groups. Blow up one balloon for each group and let them practice hitting it back and forth. See how long each group can keep the balloon in the air. Afterward, ask students to reflect on their experiences.

★ Whole-Class Activity: Keep Practicing

Watch the short YouTube video "Practice Makes Progress—Happy Monster Band" as a class and then ask students to follow the drawing prompt in the activity. Have them share their drawings with the class.

★ Journal Prompt: Practicing for the Future

Using their new understanding of practice for improvement, students will imagine what their future selves will be practicing. Then they will draw pictures of their future selves.

★ Growing Beyond

Read *Whistle for Willie* by Ezra Jack Keats as a class. Discuss how Willie kept practicing his whistle. Try whistling as a class, and encourage students to practice at home, too.

Name: _____ Date: _____

EMILY BLUNT

You may know Emily Blunt as Mary Poppins. Emily has acted in many movies.

When Emily was a child, it was hard for her to speak. Sometimes, she couldn't even say her own name!

Emily had a stutter. She struggled getting her words out.

Other kids at her school made fun of her. She was so embarrassed! Sometimes, it was easier not to speak at all.

Her parents tried to figure out why she was having trouble talking. But no one knew why.

Then one of her teachers had an idea. He saw that Emily liked to do funny voices and accents. She was good at it. And she made everyone laugh.

What if Emily tried out for the school play?

Emily was so scared! She never thought she would be able to get on stage. But her teacher asked her to try.

And it worked! When Emily was acting like she was someone else, her stutter went away.

Emily fell in love with acting. The more she practiced, the less she stuttered.

With more practice, Emily's stutter went away. She became a famous actress. She has won awards. Now, she helps other people who have a hard time talking.

Name: _____ **Date:** _____

· · · · · · · · · · · · YOU CAN IMPROVE · · · · · · · · · · · ·

With practice, we can improve on anything we want to work on. Practice helps us learn. The more we do something, the easier it gets!

Directions: After reading about Emily, what did you learn? Answer the questions below.

1. What did Emily have trouble with? _____

2. What did Emily try that helped her get over her stutter?

   _____

   _____

3. What did Emily have to do to improve?

   _____

   _____

4. What is something you would like to improve? Draw a picture of it in the box.

Name: _____ **Date:** _____

• • • • • • • • • • BALLOON TENNIS • • • • • • • • • •

Have you ever built a tower of blocks and then had it come crashing down? When the blocks fall, you build them back up again. But maybe this time, you build your tower a different way. After all, you learned something the first time.

That's what practice is all about!

In this activity, we are going to practice our skills with Balloon Tennis. It may be hard at first. But the more you practice, the easier it will become.

Directions: Your teacher will place you into groups for the game. Once you're done playing, answer the questions below.

1. What did you think of Balloon Tennis?

   _____

   _____

   _____

2. Did it get easier to play as the game went on? Why or why not?

   _____

   _____

   _____

3. What did you learn?

   _____

   _____

   _____

   _____

Name: _____   Date: _____

KEEP PRACTICING

If you have ever played a musical instrument, you know it takes some practice to learn how to play.

You can't just pick up a guitar and automatically know how to play it! First you learn a little bit about how to play it. Then you practice.

In the beginning, it might be really hard. But if you keep practicing, it will get easier.

Directions: After watching the video, think about one thing you would like to practice and improve. Draw a picture of it in the box. When you're done, share your drawing with the class.

Name: _____   Date: _____

• • • • • • • • PRACTICING FOR THE FUTURE • • • • • • • •

★ **Imagine you could go back in time to last year.**

What is one skill you have improved since then? _____

Is it something you have been practicing? _____

★ **Now, imagine you can jump forward in time to next year.**

What will you have practiced? _____

How will you have improved? _____

_____

Draw a picture of the future *you* here.

★I★ value THOUGHTFUL FEEDBACK.

> "All our dreams can come true, if we have the courage to pursue them."
>
> **Walt Disney**

Feedback helps students learn and grow. In this unit, students will learn the definition of *feedback*, and how to give and receive it.

★ Reading Passage: Walt Disney

Fired from one of his first jobs for a "lack of imagination," Walt Disney took the feedback he received and used it to make his dreams come true.

★ Short-Answer Activity: All About Feedback

Discuss the definition of *feedback* with the class, and then have students answer the comprehension questions based on the reading passage about Walt Disney.

★ Small-Group Activity: Friendly Feedback

Using the guidelines on the activity page, talk as a class about how to give feedback. Students will draw a picture on their own, and then pair up to give and receive feedback.

★ Whole-Class Activity: TAG—You're It!

Students will learn and practice a simple acronym to help them remember how to give feedback. Once complete, discuss student responses as a class and consider creating a poster with some of their responses as a visual reminder of how to give feedback.

★ Journal Prompt: Dream It, Do It

Reflecting on what they have learned about feedback, students will illustrate a dream they'd like to achieve and name the person who could help them achieve that dream.

★ Growing Beyond

Talk about receiving feedback; mirror for students how to receive constructive feedback and how they can use it to improve their work. If possible, use a personal example so students can see firsthand how it's done and why it's important.

Name: _____   Date: _____

WALT DISNEY

Have you heard of Walt Disney?

He was an artist. One of his favorite things to draw was Mickey Mouse. In fact, he invented Mickey!

Walt loved drawing. When he was young, he would sell his drawings to neighbors for some extra money.

He went to school to study art. His first job was working for a newspaper. Walt drew cartoons for them. What a fun job!

But his boss didn't like Walt's drawings. He told Walt he didn't have enough imagination. He told Walt he had "no good ideas."

Walt knew that was not true. He was filled with good ideas!

Walt and his brother Roy moved to Hollywood to start their own studio. They called it the Disney Brothers' Studio.

Soon, Walt dreamed up a cartoon about a mouse who could talk. He named him Mickey Mouse, and everyone fell in love with him.

Walt made many movies, such as *Snow White and the Seven Dwarfs*, *Mary Poppins*, and *Peter Pan*.

But he wasn't done yet. Walt had even more good ideas!

He wanted to make a theme park where people could go and meet the characters from his movies. That is how Disneyland came to be.

In the end, the feedback Walt got from his boss only helped his imagination grow even wilder!

Name: _____   **Date:** _____

⋯⋯⋯⋯⋯ ALL ABOUT FEEDBACK ⋯⋯⋯⋯⋯

⭐ **What is feedback?**

Giving feedback is telling someone what you think. It's like when a friend tells you a joke and you laugh. Your laugh is your feedback! If you cried instead, that would be a different kind of feedback.

Sometimes, when you give feedback, you are giving an idea of how someone's idea could be better.

⭐ **Why do we give feedback?**

Feedback helps us to improve.

Sometimes, others see something in our work that we missed. Or maybe they have an idea that will make it even better.

Directions: Answer the questions below.

1. How do you think Walt felt when he was told he had "no good ideas"? _____

   _____

2. How do you feel when someone gives you feedback? _____

   _____

3. Why do you feel this way? _____

   _____

   _____

   _____

   _____

   _____

   _____

Name: _____   **Date:** _____

• • • • • • • • • • • FRIENDLY FEEDBACK • • • • • • • • • • • •

Feedback should be:

⭐ Clear   ⭐ Kind   ⭐ Helpful

Here are some ways you can give feedback:

⭐ Say something nice.

⭐ Ask a question.

⭐ Give someone a new idea to make something better.

Now that you know what feedback is, you will practice with a partner.

Directions: Draw a picture in the box that goes with the sentence below. Find a partner. Bring your art with you and sit together. Decide who will go first. Share your art, and give each other feedback.

How I imagine the future will be...

Name: _____   Date: _____

TAG—YOU'RE IT!

When we give feedback, we can use TAG to remember how to do it.

⭐ **T: Tell them what they did well.**

    I really like how you…

    I loved the part…

⭐ **A: Ask a question.**

    Who? What? Where? When? Why? How?

⭐ **G: Give an idea that could make it better.**

    I wish…

    I think…

Directions: Let's practice! Answer the questions below. Then share your answers with the class.

1. What is one nice thing you could say to another student about their work?

    _____

    _____

2. What is a question you could ask someone about their work?

    _____

    _____

3. How would you tell someone you have an idea to improve their work?

    _____

    _____

Name: _____   **Date:** _____

• • • • • • • • • • • • • • DREAM IT, DO IT • • • • • • • • • • • • •

Walt Disney said, "If you can dream it, you can do it."

The feedback Walt received made him dream even bigger.

Now that you know what feedback is, can you see how it can help you improve your work?

Think about a dream that you have. Is there someone who could help you achieve your dream with their feedback?

In the box, draw a picture of what you are trying to achieve. Then write a name on the line below.

I could use feedback from _____.

I am CAPABLE of learning NEW THINGS.

> "When someone tells me I can't do something, it makes me try even harder."
>
> Ben Underwood

To learn something new, students must be willing to let go of "can't." In this unit, they will learn that the "power of yet" can help them overcome any obstacle.

★ Reading Passage: Ben Underwood

Blind since the age of three, Ben Underwood taught himself echolocation, which helped him learn to skate, surf, run, and play basketball.

★ Short-Answer Activity: Never Give Up

After reading Ben's story, students will answer comprehension questions about what they learned.

★ Small-Group Activity: I Can't Do That YET

Students will list skills or activities they haven't mastered yet on a graphic organizer and then share their work with partners.

★ Whole-Class Activity: Giraffes Can't Dance

As a class, read the book *Giraffes Can't Dance* by Giles Andreae. Students will answer questions about the story that can lead to a class discussion about reframing their mindset to discover what is possible.

★ Journal Prompt: Just Not Yet

Students are asked to write about and draw something from their list of "yets" (page 64) that they would like to work on.

★ Growing Beyond

Watch one of the short videos on *benunderwood.com* about Ben's abilities. Ask students to think about what it would be like to have to learn how to do everything they can do without the sense of sight.

Name: _____   Date: _____

BEN UNDERWOOD

Ben Underwood was born a healthy baby. But Ben was only two years old when his parents got some sad news. Ben had cancer in both of his eyes.

Ben could no longer see. He was blind.

But he found something he could do. He could click his tongue on the top of his mouth.

This clicking helped Ben hear where he was. He could hear the sound bounce off the things around him.

Ben used this clicking to help him find all kinds of things. He could tell where people were and find doorways, too.

Ben even used his clicking to learn how to do things most other blind people could not do. He could run and play basketball. He could ride a bike and a skateboard. And he could also play video games.

Ben said, "I'm not blind. I just can't see."

His parents treated him just like any other kid. His younger brother didn't even know Ben was blind at first!

Ben was able to teach himself how to do almost anything. He was never afraid of learning something new.

He traveled around the country to tell other kids his story. Ben told them to remember to never give up, even when it seems impossible!

Name: _____   **Date:** _____

NEVER GIVE UP

Even though Ben was blind, he could do many things. He was never afraid of learning how to do something new.

Directions: Think about what you learned about Ben. Then answer the questions below.

1. How did Ben "see" the world? _____

_____

_____

2. What is one thing Ben could do? _____

_____

3. What is something you learned from Ben's story? _____

_____

_____

4. What is one thing you would like to learn how to do? Draw your answer below.

Name: _____   Date: _____

• • • • • • • • • • • • • I CAN'T DO THAT YET • • • • • • • • • • • •

When something is hard or new, sometimes we tell ourselves, "I can't do that."

But there is one word you can add to that sentence that changes everything: YET.

When you say, "I can't do that YET," you are saying maybe you CAN do the thing you want to do.

Directions: Ben taught himself how to "see" without using his eyes. He never gave up, even though it was hard.

As you think about Ben's story, make lists of things you can do and things you can't do YET. Then find a partner and share your lists.

Things I Can Do

Things I Can't Do YET

Name: _____   Date: _____

GIRAFFES CAN'T DANCE

Have you ever said, "I can't do that!"? Or has someone else ever told you, "You can't do that!"?

Sometimes, all we need is a friend to help us see things in a new way.

Directions: As a class, read the book *Giraffes Can't Dance.* When you're done, answer the questions below.

1. At the beginning, what did the other animals tell Gerald?

_____

_____

_____

2. Why do you think Gerald believed them?

_____

_____

_____

3. What did the cricket say to Gerald?

_____

_____

_____

4. How do you think the cricket helped Gerald?

_____

_____

_____

Name: _____   **Date:** _____

JUST NOT YET

Directions: Choose one thing from your list of "Things I Can't Do YET" (page 64) that you would like to learn.

Draw a picture of it in this box.

What are three things you could do to help you learn this?

1. _____

   _____

2. _____

   _____

3. _____

   _____

What will it look like when you learn your "yet"? Draw a picture of it in this box.

#8309 Change Your Mindset   ©*Teacher Created Resources*

I can KEEP GOING when THINGS are TOUGH.

> "I don't need easy, I just need possible."
>
> Bethany Hamilton

It takes grit and perseverance to keep going when things get tough. In this unit, students will learn how to use grit to overcome the challenges that arise.

★ Reading Passage: Bethany Hamilton

At 13, Bethany Hamilton lost her arm in a shark attack, but she was back in the water after just a month and went on to become a professional surfer.

★ Short-Answer Activity: This Is GRIT!

Students will learn the definition of *GRIT* and reflect on what they learned from reading about Bethany Hamilton.

★ Small-Group Activity: Don't Give Up

In pairs, students will discuss what they could do instead of giving up. Then, using a graphic organizer, they will list words of encouragement they could say to themselves or each other.

★ Whole-Class Activity: A Gritty Tale

Watch the short YouTube video "Caminandes 3: Llamigos," which illustrates perseverance. Talk about what challenges the llama had to face, and how he kept going even when it got hard. Then have students follow the prompts to create a comic-strip story about grit.

★ Journal Prompt: Are You Gritty?

Students will reflect on what they have learned about grit and how they can incorporate the idea into their attitudes.

★ Growing Beyond

As a class, read *Be Unstoppable: The Art of Never Giving Up* by Bethany Hamilton or *Unstoppable Me* by Adam Dirks and Bethany Hamilton. Discuss how Bethany demonstrated grit and perseverance, and ask students what they have learned from her story.

Name: _____   **Date:** _____

· · · · · · · · · · · BETHANY HAMILTON · · · · · · · · · · ·

Bethany Hamilton has always loved the sea.

Bethany was born in Hawaii. She grew up on the island of Kauai. Everyone in her family surfed. She loved to swim and surf. She was good, too! She was so good that she started surfing in contests when she was eight.

She won a few of them. And her sights were set on winning more. But then she had an accident when she was 13.

While she was surfing one day, a shark bit her. She lost her arm.

Bethany was okay. But her family was worried. Could she still surf?

Bethany was determined to get back in the water. She was not going to let the loss of her arm stop her.

Just one month after she got out of the hospital, she was back in the water.

Bethany started surfing in contests again right away. And she won again!

She didn't quit surfing because it was harder for her with just one arm. In fact, it made her more determined to reach her goals.

Today, Bethany still loves to surf. She has written a few books about her story of never giving up. She loves to teach others how to keep going.

Name: _____ Date: _____

· · · · · · · · · · · · · · · **THIS IS GRIT!** · · · · · · · · · · · · · ·

Bethany Hamilton had to go through so much. But she never gave up on her dream of being a pro surfer. You could call this "grit."

GRIT stands for:

⭐ **G**ive it your all.

⭐ **R**edo if necessary.

⭐ **I**gnore giving up.

⭐ **T**ake time to do it right.

People with GRIT never give up, even when things get tough.

Directions: Think about Bethany's story. Then answer the questions below.

1. Do you think Bethany ever wanted to give up? Why or why not?

   _____

   _____

2. Does Bethany have GRIT? Why do you think this? _____

   _____

3. Think about a time when you wanted to give up on something. How did you feel?

   _____

4. Do you know someone else who has GRIT? Draw a picture of them in the box.

Name: _____   Date: _____

DON'T GIVE UP

What are some things you could do instead of giving up?

⭐ Take a breath.

⭐ Try again.

⭐ Try harder!

Sometimes, we need to say positive things to ourselves or one another when things get hard.

Here are some things you could say:

⭐ You've got this!

⭐ Keep going!

⭐ If you keep trying, you'll get it.

Directions: Find a partner. Talk about what you could do instead of giving up. Then make a list together. You can each write your answers on your own page.

Instead of giving up, I can...

When things get hard, I can say...

Name: _____ **Date:** _____

A GRITTY TALE

In the video, the llama was trying to get the fruit. But it wasn't easy! He had to have GRIT to get it done.

Remember what GRIT stands for:

⭐ **G**ive it your all.

⭐ **R**edo if necessary.

⭐ **I**gnore giving up.

⭐ **T**ake time to do it right.

Directions: Now, it's your turn to tell a gritty story. In the boxes below, make a comic-strip story about someone who has GRIT.

Maybe your story is about a superhero or an animal. Maybe it's about you!

Name: _____   Date: _____

· · · · · · · · · · · · ARE YOU GRITTY? · · · · · · · · · · · · ·

Now that you know all about GRIT, what will you do?

What will you do the next time you face something hard? Will you give up or try harder?

Draw a picture below of what it will look like the next time things get hard. Use the lines underneath to explain your drawing.

_____

_____

_____

_____

#8309 Change Your Mindset   ©*Teacher Created Resources*

I can TRAIN MY BRAIN.

> "I like to learn. That's an art and a science."
>
> Katherine Johnson

When students understand that our brains change as we grow, a whole new world of possibilities and potential opens up.

★ Reading Passage: Katherine Johnson

A mathematical genius, Katherine Johnson helped send the first men to the moon.

★ Short-Answer Activity: Brain Training

As they reflect on what they learned about Katherine Johnson, students will also be introduced to the idea that our brains are "muscles" that can change and grow. Then they will answer comprehension questions and share their responses with classmates.

★ Small-Group Activity: Rock or Tree?

As a class, discuss the definitions of *fixed* and *growth mindsets*, comparing *fixed* to a rock and *growth* to a tree. Then place students into pairs to complete the activity.

★ Whole-Class Activity: Your Brain Is a Muscle

Watch the short YouTube video "Growth Mindset for Students," episode 1, from ClassDojo. Talk with the class about the question posed at the end of the video. Then ask them to complete the activity.

★ Journal Prompt: I Can Train My Brain

Students will reflect on what they have learned about having a growth mindset and how it may help them going forward.

★ Growing Beyond

As a class, read *Counting on Katherine: How Katherine Johnson Put Astronauts on the Moon* by Helaine Becker. Ask students to write and draw about something they would like to train their brains to do.

Name: _____   Date: _____

KATHERINE JOHNSON

What does math have to do with going to the moon? Katherine Johnson knows the answer.

When Katherine was young, she loved to count. "I counted everything," she said. "The steps, the dishes, the stars in the sky."

Katherine had a love for math. She worked hard in school, and she went to college early.

When she was done, she had a degree in math. She went to work for NASA.

Katherine was what was called a "human computer." Before we had computers, human beings had to do all of the math.

Katherine was part of the Space Task Group. Her team figured out how to get men on the moon.

Katherine and her team used math to find out how long it would take to get there. They also figured out how fast the rocket needed to go.

Of course, counting stars is different from sending someone to the stars.

But Katherine trained her brain to do math that was harder and harder. Then one day she helped us all reach the stars!

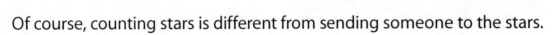

Name: _____ **Date:** _____

· · · · · · · · · · · · · · · BRAIN TRAINING · · · · · · · · · · · · · ·

Your brain is what helps you learn. And it's just like a muscle! The more you exercise your brain, the stronger it grows.

Directions: Answer the questions below. Then share your answers with at least two other students.

1. Katherine always loved to count. What is one thing that you love to do?

   _____

2. The more you use your brain, the stronger it becomes. Name one thing you could do today to exercise your brain.

   _____

   _____

3. Katherine was called a "human computer" for the work that she did. What do you think was her favorite subject in school?

   _____

4. When Katherine was a girl, there were no such things as rockets that went into space! What is one thing you can imagine that doesn't exist now but might someday? Draw a picture of it in the box.

Name: _____   **Date:** _____

· · · · · · · · · · · ROCK OR TREE? · · · · · · · · · ·

A *fixed mindset* is like a rock. It doesn't grow or change. It doesn't get bigger or smaller. It just stays a rock!

"I can't…" and "I'll never…" are *fixed-mindset* sayings.

A *growth mindset* is like a tree. It's always growing and changing. New branches and new leaves appear as it grows.

"I can keep trying!" and "I want to learn!" are *growth-mindset* sayings.

Directions: Which of the sayings below are rocks, and which are trees? Pair up with another student. Cut out the sayings at the bottom and place them where they belong.

Rock (Fixed Mindset)	Tree (Growth Mindset)

★ I will do my best.

★ This is too hard.

★ I can learn from my mistakes.

★ I can't do this.

★ I can try again!

★ I love to learn!

★ I'm not good at this.

★ I give up.

★ I can't do this YET!

Name: _____   **Date:** _____

· · · · · · · · · YOUR BRAIN IS A MUSCLE · · · · · · · · ·

In the video, Mojo discovers that the brain is a muscle.

That means that mistakes are like lifting weights! We have to lift weights to make our muscles stronger. So our mistakes can help us get stronger, too.

We also learn by connecting what we already know to new information. That also makes our brains stronger!

Directions: What are some other ways you can think of that would help your brain get stronger? List your ideas here.

★ _____

_____

★ _____

_____

★ _____

_____

★ _____

_____

★ _____

_____

Name: _____ **Date:** _____

· · · · · · · · · · I CAN TRAIN MY BRAIN · · · · · · · · · ·

Katherine Johnson said, "I'm always interested in learning something new." That is having a growth mindset!

Write your answers to the questions below.

⭐ **Do you have a growth mindset? How do you know?** ⭐

⭐ **What is your favorite thing you have learned about being able to train your brain?** ⭐

⭐ **How will having a growth mindset help you?** ⭐

MEETING STANDARDS

Most of the activities in *Change Your Mindset: Growth Mindset Activities for the Classroom* meet one or more of the following Common Core State Standards © Copyright 2010. National Governors Association Center for Best Practices and Council of Chief State School Officers. All rights reserved. For more information about the Common Core State Standards, go to *http://www.corestandards.org/* or *http://www.teachercreated.com/standards/*.

Grade 1	
Reading: Informational Text	**Activity Title (Unit #)**
Key Ideas and Details	
ELA.RI.1.1: Ask and answer questions about key details in a text.	The Best You Can Be (1), Great Effort (2), Learning from Mistakes (3), I Believe in Myself (4), Big Dreams (5), Challenged to Grow (6), Growing Beyond (6), Creativity Counts (7), You Can Improve (8), Never Give Up (10), This Is GRIT! (11), Brain Training (12)
Range of Reading and Level of Text Complexity	
ELA.RI.1.10: With prompting and support, read informational texts appropriately complex for grade 1.	Misty Copeland (1), Michael Jordan (2), Thomas Edison (3), Bindi Irwin (4), Kwame Alexander (5), Albert Einstein (6), Growing Beyond (6), Mo Willems (7), Help Is on the Way! (7), Growing Beyond (7), Emily Blunt (8), Walt Disney (9), Ben Underwood (10), Bethany Hamilton (11), Growing Beyond (11), Katherine Johnson (12), Growing Beyond (12)
Writing	**Activity Title (Unit #)**
Text Types and Purposes	
ELA.W.1.3: Write narratives in which they recount two or more appropriately sequenced events, include some details regarding what happened, use temporal words to signal event order, and provide some sense of closure.	Doing Your Best (1), Have Some Courage (6), Growing Beyond (7), A Gritty Tale (11)
Research to Build and Present Knowledge	
ELA.W.1.8: With guidance and support from adults, recall information from experiences or gather information from provided sources to answer a question.	The Best You Can Be (1), Best of Friends (1), Doing Your Best (1), Great Effort (2), Giving Your Best (2), Learning from Mistakes (3), Taught by Mistake (3), I Believe in Myself (4), I Can Do Anything (4), Big Dreams (5), Stars & Wishes (5), Reaching for the Stars (5), Challenged to Grow (6), Have Some Courage (6), Creativity Counts (7), Help Is on the Way! (7), You Can Improve (8), Practicing for the Future (8), All About Feedback (9), Giraffes Can't Dance (10), Just Not Yet (10), This Is GRIT! (11), Brain Training (12), Your Brain Is a Muscle (12), I Can Train My Brain (12)
Speaking & Listening	**Activity Title (Unit #)**
Comprehension and Collaboration	
ELA.SL.1.1: Participate in collaborative conversations with diverse partners about *grade 1 topics and texts* with peers and adults in small and larger groups.	Best of Friends (1), Great Effort (2), Your Best (2), Growing Beyond (2), We Made This! (3), Growing Beyond (3), I Believe in Myself (4), Stars & Wishes (5), Go for the Goal (5), Have Some Courage (6), Being Brave (6), Help Is on the Way! (7), Friendly Feedback (9), TAG—You're It! (9), I Can't Do That YET (10), Don't Give Up (11), Growing Beyond (11), Brain Training (12)
Presentation of Knowledge and Ideas	
ELA.SL.1.4: Describe people, places, things, and events with relevant details, expressing ideas and feelings clearly.	Best of Friends (1), Great Effort (2), Growing Beyond (3), I Believe in Myself (4), Reflection of Me (4), Stars & Wishes (5), Go for the Goal (5), Help Is on the Way! (7), Balloon Tennis (8), Don't Give Up (11), Brain Training (12)

Grade 2

Reading: Informational Text	Activity Title (Unit #)
Key Ideas and Details	
ELA.RI.2.1: Ask and answer such questions as *who, what, where, when, why,* and *how* to demonstrate understanding of key details in a text.	The Best You Can Be (1), Great Effort (2), Learning from Mistakes (3), I Believe in Myself (4), Big Dreams (5), Challenged to Grow (6), Growing Beyond (6), Creativity Counts (7), You Can Improve (8), Never Give Up (10), This Is GRIT! (11), Brain Training (12)
Range of Reading and Level of Text Complexity	
ELA.RI.2.10: By the end of year, read and comprehend informational texts, including history/social studies, science, and technical texts, in the grades 2–3 text complexity band proficiently, with scaffolding as needed at the high end of the range.	Misty Copeland (1), Michael Jordan (2), Thomas Edison (3), Bindi Irwin (4), Kwame Alexander (5), Albert Einstein (6), Growing Beyond (6), Mo Willems (7), Help Is on the Way! (7), Growing Beyond (7), Emily Blunt (8), Walt Disney (9), Ben Underwood (10), Bethany Hamilton (11), Growing Beyond (11), Katherine Johnson (12), Growing Beyond (12)

Writing	Activity Title (Unit #)
Text Types and Purposes	
ELA.W.2.3: Write narratives in which they recount a well-elaborated event or short sequence of events, include details to describe actions, thoughts, and feelings, use temporal words to signal event order, and provide a sense of closure.	Doing Your Best (1), Have Some Courage (6), Growing Beyond (7), A Gritty Tale (11)
Research to Build and Present Knowledge	
ELA.W.2.8: Recall information from experiences or gather information from provided sources to answer a question.	The Best You Can Be (1), Best of Friends (1), Doing Your Best (1), Great Effort (2), Giving Your Best (2), Learning from Mistakes (3), Taught by Mistake (3), I Believe in Myself (4), I Can Do Anything (4), Big Dreams (5), Stars & Wishes (5), Go for the Goal (5), Reaching for the Stars (5), Challenged to Grow (6), Have Some Courage (6), Creativity Counts (7), Help Is on the Way! (7), You Can Improve (8), Practicing for the Future (8), All About Feedback (9), Giraffes Can't Dance (10), Just Not Yet (10), This Is GRIT! (11), Brain Training (12), Your Brain Is a Muscle (12), I Can Train My Brain (12)

Speaking & Listening	Activity Title (Unit #)
Comprehension and Collaboration	
ELA.SL.2.1: Participate in collaborative conversations with diverse partners about *grade 2 topics and texts* with peers and adults in small and larger groups.	Best of Friends (1), Great Effort (2), Your Best (2), Growing Beyond (2), We Made This! (3), Growing Beyond (3), I Believe in Myself (4), Stars & Wishes (5), Go for the Goal (5), Have Some Courage (6), Being Brave (6), Help Is on the Way! (7), Friendly Feedback (9), TAG—You're It! (9), I Can't Do That YET (10), Don't Give Up (11), Growing Beyond (11), Brain Training (12)
Presentation of Knowledge and Ideas	
ELA.SL.2.4: Tell a story or recount an experience with appropriate facts and relevant, descriptive details, speaking audibly in coherent sentences.	Best of Friends (1), Great Effort (2), Growing Beyond (3), I Believe in Myself (4), Reflection of Me (4), Stars & Wishes (5), Go for the Goal (5), Help Is on the Way! (7), Balloon Tennis (8), Don't Give Up (11), Brain Training (12)